A long time ago, as a little girl,
I dreamed of traveling all over the world

And often I'd ask about the past
Driving everyone crazy fast!

Amused by this my parents thought,
Why not call me "History" for short?

Since then I've traveled
By land, sea, and air ...

Little Miss HISTORY Travels to
INTREPID Sea, Air & Space Museum
© 2015 Barbara Ann Mojica. All Rights Reserved.

Published in The UNITED STATES of AMERICA
eugenus® STUDIOS, LLC
P.O. BOX 112
CRARYVILLE, NY 12521
E-Mail: Barbara@LittleMissHistory.com
WebSite: www.LittleMissHISTORY.com

ISBN-13: 978-0-9885030-3-8
ISBN-10: 0988503034

Barbara Ann Mojica's

Little Miss HISTORY® Travels to

INTREPID
Sea, Air & Space Museum

Illustrations by VICTOR RAMON MOJICA

Today we are traveling by sea,
air and Space all at one place.

We are on the
INTREPID Sea,
Air & Space Museum.
She's on the Hudson
River at Pier 86 in
New York City.

The *USS Intrepid* was commissioned on August 8th, 1943, to serve in World War II.

Vice Admiral Thomas Lamison Sprague served as *Intrepid's* first captain.

Her crew adopted the motto
In Mare In Coelo,
("In the Sea In Heaven" or
"On the Sea (and) In the Sky").

In October of 1944, the *Intrepid* fought in the largest battle in US naval history at Leyte Gulf, Philippines helping to sink the super-battleship *Musashi*.

Many other enemy ships and planes were destroyed during that three day battle.

Japanese pilots who crashed their planes into enemy ships intentionally were called Kamikazes.

On October 29th, 1944,
nineteen year old
Alonzo Swann Jr.
and twenty-two other
black sailors, fought off
a Kamikaze attack.

The kamikaze's fiery debris injured some while killing others in Alonzo's group ...

... but in the fire and confusion, Alonzo stayed at his post trying to save his shipmates.

He and the five other surviving African American gunners received only the Bronze Star.

Fifty years later Alonzo Swann received the highest naval military honor, the Navy Cross.

By the end of World War II,
Intrepid earned the title of ...

... "The Navy's Most Frequently Hit Carrier."

Naval engineers modernized the *Intrepid* in the 1950's.
In May of 1962, she began serving ...

... as a recovery vessel for NASA
(National Aeronautics and Space Administration).

On March 23rd, 1965, *Intrepid* recovered astronauts Gus Grissom and John Young in their Gemini 3 spacecraft, *Molly Brown.*

Intrepid remained an attack carrier
until 1962, when she became
an antisubmarine warfare carrier.

She tracked Russian submarines during the Cold War.

Cold Wars are fought with words instead of weapons.

Intrepid served three tours off Vietnam in 1966 hitting targets in the Gulf of Tonkin ...

... earning one of the fastest launching times recorded by an American carrier.

Intrepid's commanding officer at the time, Captain John W. Fair, won the Legion of Merit medal for combat operations.

On March 15th, 1974,
Intrepid was decommissioned
for the final time.

Four years later, retired Admiral Zachary Fisher and his wife, Elizabeth, found *Intrepid* in a scrap yard.

They spent $24 million of their own money to save the once mighty warship.

In 1982, *Intrepid* moved to New York City and opened as a museum.

Her mission today is to honor our veteran fighters, teach the public, and inspire young people.

Intrepid's flight deck holds many different types of aircraft ...

... fighter jets, supersonic jets, and helicopters, to name just a few.

You can get a close look at
the Space Shuttle *Enterprise*.
She sits inside her own bubble
on *Intrepid's* flight deck.

Visit the Exploreum below the flight deck ...

... and learn what it's like to live on an aircraft carrier.

Watch war movies of past history.

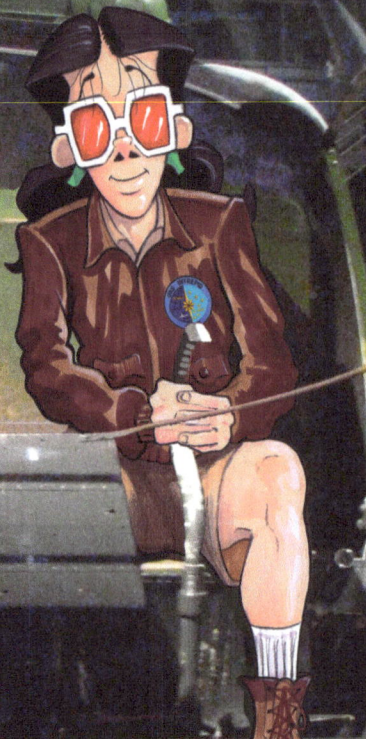

Have some fun
in Exploreum's
Interactive Hall.

The *Growler* Submarine
is docked right next door
to the *Intrepid*.
You can even go inside.

Here are samples of
what you will see ...

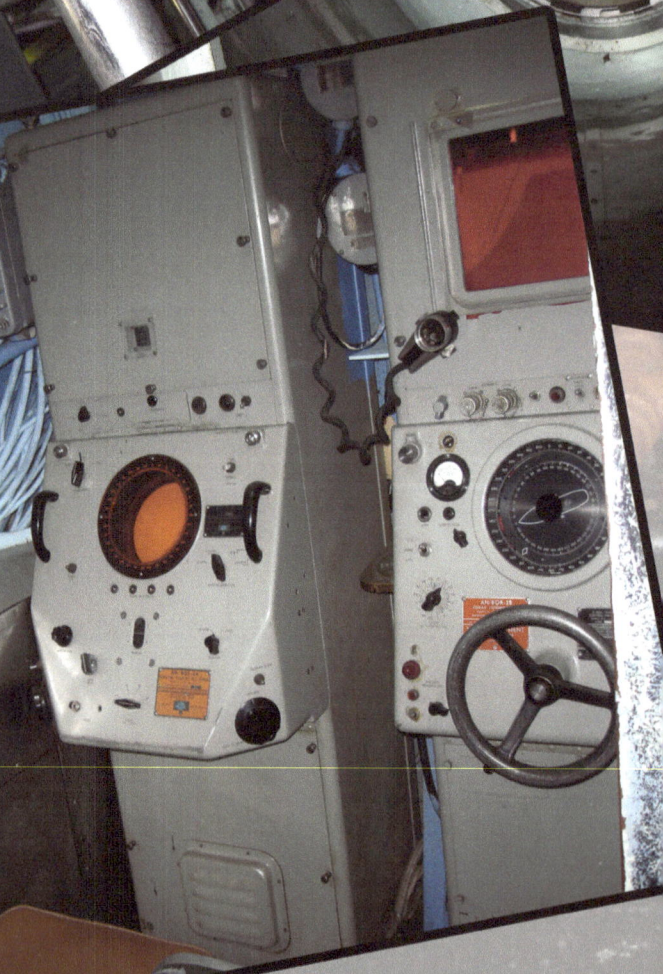

RESTRICTED AREA

Intrepid played a new role after September 11th, 2001 in New York City.

She served as temporary
field headquarters for
750 FBI agents
investigating the
World Trade Center
terrorist attack.

I am humbled in honoring
the heroes who served on *Intrepid*,
one of the most successful ships
in US naval history.

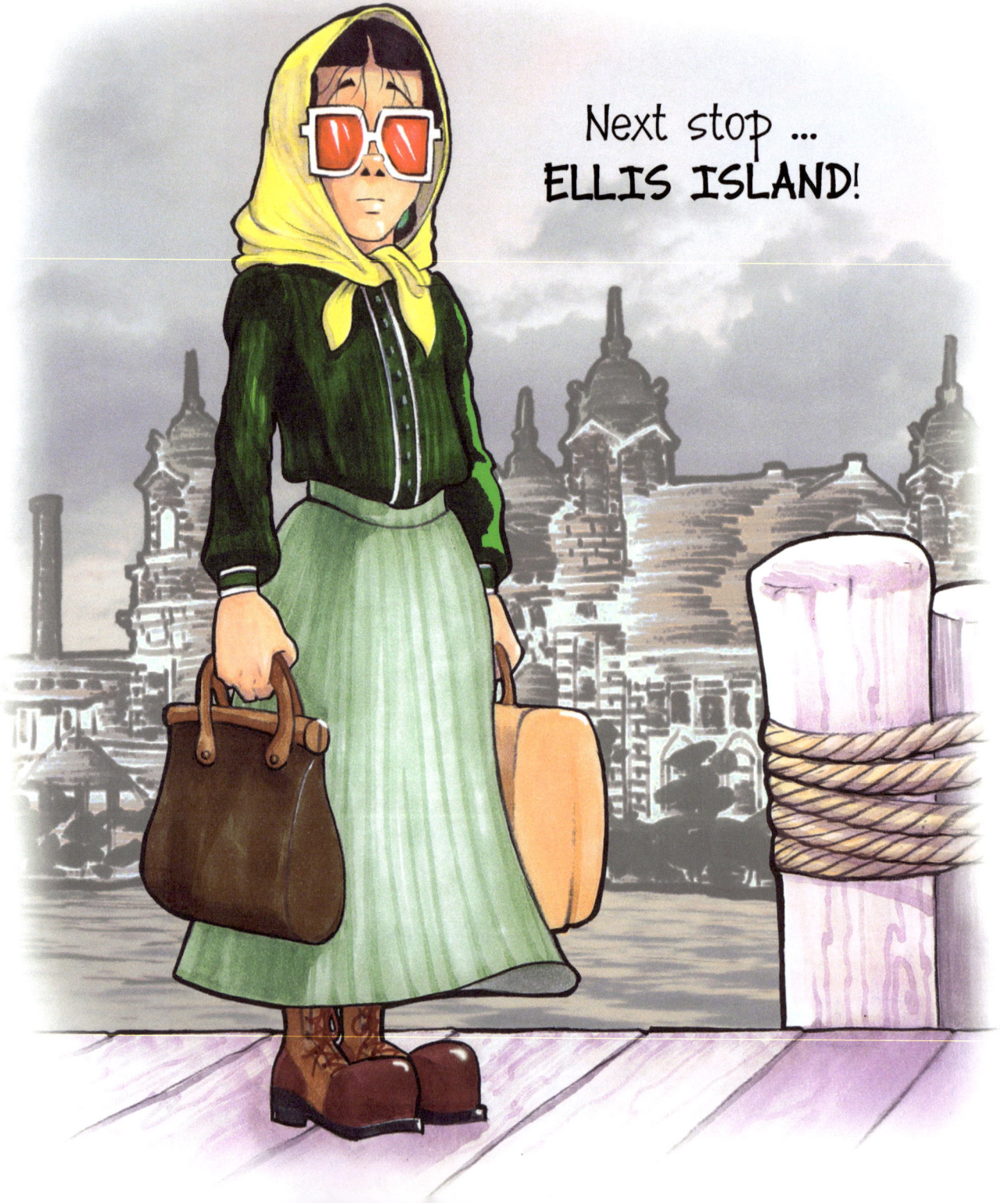

www.ingramcontent.com/pod-product-compliance
Lightning Source LLC
Chambersburg PA
CBHW042058040426
42448CB00002B/58